Anonymous

**Questions for the Classes of Trades School of the**

**Massachusetts Reformatory**

Anonymous

**Questions for the Classes of Trades School of the Massachusetts Reformatory**

ISBN/EAN: 9783337296377

Printed in Europe, USA, Canada, Australia, Japan

Cover: Foto ©Suzi / pixelio.de

More available books at **www.hansebooks.com**

MASSACHUSETTS REFORMATORY.

# QUESTIONS

FOR THE

# PLUMBING CLASS

## NO. I.

REFORMATORY PRINT
1896.

# QUESTIONS.

1. Name the tools used in plumbing?

2. What is solder made out of?

3. What is lead tax made from?

4. Name the exercises in plumbing?

5. How would you tin a soldering iron?

6. What is used besides solder to make a cup joint?

7. Only what metals is it proper to use acid on?

8. What is the average size of pipe used for water service in a house?

9. Name the different sizes in lead pipe and their weights per foot?

10. Where is sink located in a house?

11. Where are laundry tubs located?

12. Where are bath tub, water-closet and set wash bowl located?

13. Is it proper to use acid on lead connections?

14. What is the difference between wiping solder and fine solder, same as used with iron?

15. How would you clean solder?

16. What is needed to wipe a joint with?

17. What are wiping cloths made from?

18. What are the sizes of wiping cloths?

19. Name the different wiping cloths?

20. How do you prepare a lead pipe to join it together, joint to be wiped?

21. How do you prepare a bolt joint?

22. How do you prepare an overcast joint?

23. How do you prepare a joint to wipe on a faucet?

24. What is used to prevent solder from sticking all over pipes?

25. What is used to form a nice straight edge on round joint?

# QUESTIONS

FOR THE

# PLUMBING CLASS.

## NO. 2.

# NOTES.

Before commencing work understand how each line of pipe is to be placed and where each connection is to be made. Make a diagram of each line of pipe with its connections drawn to a scale. This will save money by saving time and avoiding waste of material.

Do not use inferior material to secure a job or even to oblige the owner. The loss of reputation, which, in the end will ensue, will more than equal any profit which may be obtained.

A leak in a soil pipe may cause death or the ruin of a life through sickness.

As cast iron pipe depends for its strength and for freedom from flaws and sand-holes upon the soundness of the casting, it is best to deal with houses of established reputation only. Tarred pipe is the most durable, but the tar temporarily covers imperfections in the casting.

# QUESTIONS.

1. What kind of pipe is used for drainage and waste water?

2. Is ventilation a benefit to house drainage?

3. What part of a trap should the ventilation be taken from?

4. Why is it that a fresh air vent is not practical unless carried above the highest window in the house?

5. What does syphoning a trap mean?

6. What size soil pipe is used mostly where there are six fixtures perpendicularly? Water-closets and bowls?

7. What size soil pipe leading from a bath-room to drain should be used in order to get a proper flush?

8. Is it proper to have a separate trap for bath-tub?

9. Is it proper to have a separate trap for wash-bowl?

10.  In order to prevent traps under fixtures from syphonage what should be done?

11.  How much seal of water has a water-closet trap got?

12.  How much seal of water has a 1 1-2 full S trap for sink?

13.  How much seal of water has a round trap got?

14.  Why is it that a round trap is not as practical as a full S trap?

15.  What size lead may be used for waste for sinks and bowls?

16.  What kind of a faucet is best to use over a urinal?

17.  Why is it the best?

18.  What is a cleanout in a drain?

19.  What causes expansion and contraction in water pipes?

20.  What is a running trap, and what is it used for?

21. Is it proper to run conductors into drain?

22. How would you connect cast iron pipe joints together?

23. How would you run a joint in iron pipe when the pipe runs horizontally?

24. What does calking a joint mean?

25. What is a lead pipe fastened by when upright against a wall?

26. What is it fastened by when running across ceiling or side walls.

27. What is soil pipe fastened by to wall when running upright.

28. Name the different fittings used with 4 inch soil pipe?

29. What is a tank used for?

30. What is a water-closet valve?

31. How is it operated?

32. Describe what a ball cock is?

33. What is it used for?

34. How large should a pipe from tank to water-closet be in order to get a good flush?

35. How high should an ordinary size tank be from floor to get a good flush?

36. What is a trap and why is it used?

37. Name the different traps in ordinary use?

38. Do they always allow the waste from sink to enter drain without catching greasy matter?

39. Why is it they use a catch basin or a grease trap?

40. Name the tools needed to connect soil pipe?

41. Where is stop-cock placed to control water from going up through the house to fixtures?

42. Is there more than one stop-cock required in a modern improved house?

43. Name the fixtures connected with modern improvements?

44. Is it best not to enclose plumbing work from sight? And why?

45. What is a shower bath?

46. How is it arranged and where in the bath-room?

47. In order to get a good flow of hot water in house where should tank be located?

48. What care should be taken when arranging tank in above position?

49. Is it necessary for a plumber to understand plans?

50. What is the best way to test soil pipe?

# QUESTIONS

## FOR THE

# TINSMITH CLASS.

# QUESTIONS.

1. What tools are generally used in this trade?

2. What are used for bench tools?

3. How many kinds of snips and shears are used?

4. How many hammers?

5. What are the names of machines used by tinsmiths?

6. Describe the use of each.

7. What stakes are used?

8. Name the use of each.

9. What is a lap-seam?

10. What is a groove?

11. What is a double seam?

12. What metals are commonly worked in this trade?

13. Name the different tins, and how they differ.

14. How are the different weights of tin expressed?

15. Which is the thicker, X or XX, etc.?

16. What is meant by charcoal tin?

17. What by coke tin?

18. What by terne tin?

19. What by Banca tin?

20. What by straits tin?

21. How many kinds of iron are used in this trade?

22. How is the weight expressed on American iron.

23. How on American galvanized?

24. How on Russia iron?

25. What iron is best?

26. What is the most expensive, and why?

27. What the least expensive?

28. What is the difference in appearance?

29. Name the different kinds of copper usually worked in this trade.

30. What is meant by hard and soft copper?

31. What by planished copper?

32. What by tinned copper?

33. What by plain copper?

34. What by bolt copper?

35. Name some of the uses of each.

36. How many kinds of zinc do we use?

37. Name some of the places in which zinc is better than iron (either plain or galvanized).

38. Why is zinc preferable to iron for roofs and valleys on roofs, etc.?

39. Why is zinc usually put under stoves instead of iron or tin?

40. Of what is solder composed?

41. What proportions?

42. When solder shrinks in cooling is it too coarse, or fine?

43. What is meant by coarse, or fine?

44. How do you improve it if too coarse?

45. How, if too fine?

46. What do you use in soldering?

47. Why is resin used in soldering?

48. Why is muriatic acid used?

49. How do you prepare a soldering copper for use?

50. How do you prepare iron for soldering?

51. How tin?

52. How zinc?

53. How lead?

54. What will melt at least heat, iron or solder?

55. What melts first, brass or solder?

56. What melts first, zinc or solder?

# QUESTIONS

## ABOUT

# Brickwork, Lime, Mortar and Cement.

## FOR BRICKLAYING CLASS.

# BRICKWORK.

Bond is an arrangement of bricks or stones laid beside and above each other, so that the vertical joints between any two bricks does not coincide with that between any other two. (This is termed "breaking joints").

Header is a brick laid with an end to face of wall.

Stretcher is a brick laid parallel to face of wall.

Header Course or Bond is a course or courses of headers alone.

Closers are pieces of bricks inserted in alternate courses, in order to obtain a bond by preventing two headers from being exactly over a stretcher.

Flemish Bond is laying of headers and stretchers alternately in each course.

Guaged Work—Bricks cut and rubbed to exact shape required.

String Course is a horizontal and projecting course around a building.

Cornice is a projection which crowns or finishes the parts of a building.

Color of Bricks depends upon composition of the

clay, the moulding sand, temperature of burning and volume of air admitted to kiln.

Pure clay, that is free from iron, will burn white.

Presence of iron produces a tint ranging from red and orange to a light yellow, according to proportion of iron.

Why should bricks always be wet before being used?

Because a dry brick will absorb the water from the mortar and will become a powdery mass of lime and sand and injure the binding power of the mortar.

To find the number of bricks required for a building or wall.

Find the number of cubic feet by multiplying the length, height and thickness of walls (in feet) together. This multiplied by 22 1-2 (the number of bricks in a cubic foot) will be the number of bricks required.

To find the number of bricks in a wall.

First ascertain the number of square feet of surface, and then multiply by seven for a 4-inch wall, by 14 for an 8-inch wall, by 21 for a 12-inch wall, and by 28 for a 16-inch wall.

Above rules are for bricks 8 inches long, 4 inches wide, and 2 inches thick.

# Questions About Lime, Mortar and Cement.

1. How is lime obtained?

   By calcining limestone.

2. What is meant by calcining?

   Expelling the moisture and the carbonic acid gas from the limestone by action of heat, moisture and carbonic acid gas being component parts of limestone.

3. What is carbonic acid gas?

   It is poisonous; it is found in the atmosphere; it is thrown off in large quantities of decaying vegetable matter; it is produced by our breath and from burning charcoal; it can be obtained from limestone by pouring sulphuric acid upon it.

4. What happens when lime is exposed to the air?

   It becomes air slaked.

5. What is meant by air slaked?

   Lime which, when exposed to the air, absorbs moisture and carbonic acid. This makes it unfit for mortar, because it is necessary that the carbonic acid gas be absorbed after the mortar is used.

6. How is mortar made?

   Mortar is made by mixing one part of slaked lime to two parts of clean, sharp sand.

7. How much water does lime absorb in slaking?
   About one-quarter its weight.

8. How much does lime expand when mixed with water?

   Two or three times.

9. What sort of sand is the best for mortar?
   Clean, sharp sand.

10. How can sand be tested?

    By rubbing it on the palm of the hand. It should scratch the skin, but not soil it.

11. Why is sea sand objectionable?

    It has had its angles worn off by friction, and it is impregnated with salt.

12. What harm does the salt do?

    Salt absorbs water. Mortar in which salt enters is constantly becoming damp. by absorbing moisture from the atmosphere.

13. Will slaked lime keep without being mixed with water?

    Yes; slaked lime, so long as it is protected from the atmosphere, is benefited by being kept, any impurities existing in it become absorbed.

The Roman building laws required it to be kept two years. In Italy the lime is always slaked when a building is commenced and kept in pits, covered with a layer of earth. When the slaked lime cracks, the earth is scraped off and the lime is sprinkled and covered again. It is kept covered with earth to prevent the absorption of the carbonic acid gas from the atmosphere.

14. How should slaked lime and sand be mixed to make mortar?

It should be mixed so thoroughly that each grain of sand is covered with a thin film of slaked lime, and a sufficient quantity of slaked lime added to make a paste like moss.

15. What should be particularly guarded against?

That no lumps of unslaked lime or masses of sand unmixed with lime should be left; both are injurious to the mortar.

16. Is there any advantage in keeping mortar after it is mixed with sand?

Rather the reverse. As it commences to harden the only advantage is that the second working mixes the lime and sand as thoroughly as should have been done at first.

17. Why is mortar more adhesive than slaked lime unmixed with sand?

Slaked lime, when dried in any quantity, will easily crumble, and also shrinks considerably as it dries.

18. When hair is added to mortar for plastering, what precaution must be taken?

The mortar must be cold, otherwise the hair will be burned and the plaster will be liable to fall.

19. How does mortar unite bricks?

By entering into the pores of the bricks and forming a solid mass with the bricks.

20. How are cements divided?

. They are divided into two classes—natural and artificial cement.

21. What is natural cement?

Cement made from limestone containing about 20 per cent. of clay. Rosendale cement is a natural cement, and is from Rosendale, N. Y.

22. Name some of the artificial cements?

Hydraulic, Roman and Portland cement.

23. What is hydraulic cement used mostly for?

It is used in construction of fortifications, break-waters, foundations of bridges, etc., because of the useful properties which it possesses of rapidly settling when immersed in water.

24. What are some of the properties of Hydraulic cement?

The best of Hydraulic cement contains a large proportion of silica, alumina and magnesia. It does not slake after calcination, and will set under water in from 3 to 4 minutes, while others require as many hours. It does not shrink in hardening, and makes an excellent mortar without any admixture of sand.

25. What is Roman cement?

It is made from a lime of peculiar character found in England and France, and derived from kidney shaped stones. It is about 33 per cent. of the strength of Portland, and is not adapted for use with sand.

26. What is Portland cement?

It is made in England and France from chalk and clay; this mixture is moulded into bricks burned in a kiln at a low temperature to expel the carbonic acid gas, and is ground to a powder. Portland cement is improved by age if kept from moisture. It possesses the advantage of being managed by ordinary workmen. As quick setting cement is always difficult to use, it requires special workmen and an active supervision. The less water used in mixing cement the better. Bricks, stones, etc., used with cement should be well wet before used. In using sand with cement, at the end of a year 1 of cement to 1 of sand is about 75 per cent. of the strength of neat cement; 1 to 2, 50 per cent. strength; 1 to 3, 33 per cent. strength; 1 to 4, 25 per cent. strength; 1 to 5, 16 per cent. strength. The above requires clean and sharp sand. Salt water has a tendency to decompose cement of all kinds, and its strength is considerably impaired by a mixture with it.

# QUESTIONS

FOR THE

# BLACKSMITH CLASS.

# QUESTIONS.

1. How should a forge be built?

2. How should a chimney be built?

3. What kind of a tuyere iron should be used?

4. Why are bellows or blowers used?

5. What is the difference between anthracite and bituminous coal?

6. What kind of coal is used in a forge?

7. Why is this kind used?

8. What is coke?

9. What is charcoal?

10. When is charcoal used in blacksmithing?

11. Why should it be used?

12. How should a fire be built?

13. Why should we wet coal?

14. Describe the following-named tools and their uses:
Flat and round pein hammers, sledge, tongs

hardy, cutter, cold chisel, centre punch, punch, calipers, rule, top and bottom swages, top and bottom fullers, heading tools, vise.

15. What are stakes and small horns used for?

16. How should an anvil be made?

17. What metals do blacksmiths use?

18. Where do we get iron?

19. How is it prepared for use?

20. What are the different grades of iron?

21. What makes some kinds of iron so much better than others?

22. Why does iron work easier when heated?

23. What is meant by upsetting iron?

24. What is meant by chamfer?

25. What is meant by an offset?

26. What is meant by welding iron?

27. What is a scarf?

28. How many kinds of welds are there?

29. Explain the scarfs for the different welds?

30. Why is sand used in welding? .

31. Why is iron upset before welding?

32. What is solid work?

33. How is steel made?

34. What is the difference between cheap steel and fine steel?

35. What kind of a fire should be used for steel work?

36. Why does it spoil steel to overheat it?

37. How hot should steel be heated?

38. How is steel tempered?

39. What makes the color?

40. How do we know what color to use?

41. Why not cool the steel at a certain heat and get the same result?

42. What color should be used to temper a tool to cut iron?

43. What color should be used to temper a tool to cut steel?

44. What color should be used to temper a tool to cut stone?

45. What color should be used to temper a tool to cut wood?

46. Why is a tool tempered harder to cut wood than · steel?

47. What kind of steel is used for tool making?

48. What is low grade steel used for?

49. Why are some tools made of iron and steel faced?

50. Explain all about welding steel, and why borax is used?

# QUESTIONS

### FOR THE

## CLASS IN

# CARPENTRY.

# QUESTIONS.

1.  Name some of the most important bench tools.

2.  Explain the marks and figures on a two-foot rule.

3.  Name the different kinds of bench planes.

4.  What is the jack plane used for mostly?

5.  What plane is used to joint and straighten edges and surfaces of boards, etc.?

6.  Which plane is used to smooth this work?

7.  What is the block plane used for?

8.  Name some of the different kinds of saws.

9.  What is the cross-cut saw used for?

10.  Which saw is used to cut lengthwise with the grain?

11.  How should the file be held to file a cross-cut saw?

12.  How should the file be held to file a splitting saw?

13. What is a steel square?

14. What is a try square and what is it used for?

15. Explain the use of the guage.

16. Explain a use of the bevel.

17. What is a witness or try mark?

18. In working boards to a certain length and breadth and thickness what tools do you use?

19. What will give the best results planing with or against the grain?

20. Explain the exercise of planing a board to a certain length, breadth and thickness.

21. What is meant by square joints?

22. Explain a mitre joint.

23. How do you set a bevel for a mitre on the steel square?

24. What is a mortise and tenon joint?

25. Explain the dove tail and blind dove tail joints.

26. Explain the use of the mitre box.

27. What is meant by board measure?

28. How many feet in a board 12 feet long, 12 in. wide and 1 in. thick?

29. What is meant by joist?

30. Name some of the different sizes of joist.

31. Name some of the principal parts of a frame of a wooden building.

32. What are sills and cross sills?

33. What are floor joist headers and bridging?

34. What are posts braces and studding?

35. What are plate rafters and ridge?

36. What are partitions and partition caps?

37. How should the sills of a house be placed?

38. How can you square the sill by the use of a 10 foot pole?

39. What kinds of wood are mostly used for the frames of a wooden building?

40. What is used for boarding sides and roofing?

41.   What is used for outside finish mostly?

42.   Give some of the names for outside finish.

43.   What are matched boards?

44.   What is blind nailing on matched boards?

45.   What is a panel?

46.   Name the different joints in a panel door.

47.   Name the different parts in a panel door?

48.   What is a raised panel?

49.   What is a raised moulding?

50.   What is a flush moulding?

51.   Name some of the different sizes of nails.

52.   What is the difference between brads and common nails?

# QUESTIONS.

1. Name the tools used in plumbing.

2. What is solder made out of?

3. What is lead tax made from?

4. Name the exercises in plumbing.

5. How would you tin a soldering iron?

6. What is used beside solder to make a cup joint?

7. Only what metals is it proper to use acid on?

8. What is the average size of pipe used for water service in a house?

9. Name the different sizes in lead pipe and their weights per foot.

10. Where is sink located in a house?

11. Where are laundry tubs located?

12. Where are bath tub, water-closer and set wash bowl located?

13. Is it proper to use acids on lead connections?

14. What is the difference between wiping solder and fine solder, same as used with iron?

15. How would you clean solder?

16. What is needed to wipe a joint with?

17. What are wiping cloths made from?

18. What are the sizes of wiping cloths?

19. Name the different wiping cloths.

20. How do you prepare a lead pipe to joint it together, joint to be wiped?

21. How do you prepare a bolt joint?

22. How do you prepare an over cast joint?

23. How do you prepare a joint to wipe on a faucet?

24. What is used to prevent solder from sticking all
over pipes?

25. What is used to form a nice straight edge on
round joint?